D1587720

FERRARI CABRIOLETS & SPYDERS

Osprey AutoHistory

FERRARI CABRIOLETS & SPYDERS

166 Inter to Mondial Quattrovalvole

JONATHAN THOMPSON

Published in 1985 by Osprey Publishing Limited
12–14 Long Acre, London WC2E 9LP
Member company of the George Philip Group

Sole distributors for the USA

Publishers & Wholesalers Inc
Osceola, Wisconsin 54020, USA

British Library Cataloguing in Publication Data

Thompson, Jonathan
    Ferrari Cabriolets & Spyders—(AutoHistory)
    1. Ferrari automobile
    I. Title   II. Series
    629.2'222   TL212.F47
ISBN 0-85045-553-7

Editor Tim Parker
Picture research by the author

Filmset in Great Britain
Printed in England by BAS Printers, Over Wallop

Contents

Introduction

This book covers all road Ferraris with retractable or removable tops. It does not cover open two-seaters built for competition use, although in the case of the earliest Ferraris the distinction is hard to make.

Perhaps the most accurate title would employ the American term: *Ferrari convertibles*. The English term 'drophead' doesn't apply consistently, considering that many modern Ferraris have removable hardtops or Targa roof panels. The French world *cabriolet* (originally applied to a one-horse carriage with a folding top, and deriving from the Latin word for goat, specifically its bounding motion) is used internationally, almost universally denoting a four-seater car with a disappearing soft-top. The German and Italian designation *spyder* (or *spider*) generally means a more sporting two-seater car, equivalent to what is called a roadster or speedster in English-speaking countries. But a spyder can be a competition machine with a small windscreen and no top whatsoever, a road car with a folding top and side curtains or wind-up windows, or in its most modern configuration, a Targa (a name coined by Porsche) with steel rollbar, fixed rear window and removable panel or panels above the cockpit. These days it is likely to have electric windows, a complex stereo system and, yes, even air conditioning! Is there no shame?

Although the numbers have been small compared to the total factory production, open-air Ferraris have been continually if not continuously available. With the falling off of convertible production worldwide during the 1970s, the soft-top Ferrari disappeared temporarily. But when something is scarce it usually increases in value. Genuine open Ferraris have commanded prices well above those of their berlinetta or coupé equivalents, and a cottage industry of convertible conversions has sprung up among Ferrari specialists in England, the United States, Germany and Italy. Some of the conversions have duplicated faithfully the design and quality of the authentic originals, others less so, and still others have involved significant restyling and completely new variations.

The point was that Ferrari enthusiasts were hungry for the open models. The factory increased production of the GTS version of its 308 (to the extent that this model now outnumbers all previous open Ferraris combined) and introduced a cabriolet version of its Mondial 8 (let it be said, a none-too-popular model in coupé form), with a true folding top. While major manufacturers have not returned to convertible production in any significant numbers, the interest in open cars has been rekindled worldwide, providing an ideal market for the smaller specialist firms.

In the late 1940s, when Enzo Ferrari began to sell road cars to private customers as a means to underwrite his extensive racing programme, the available models could be roughly divided into two groups. Competition spyders and berlinettas, with very lightweight bodywork by such *carrozzerie* as Touring, Allemano and Vignale, were sold to those clients who wished to go racing. More sedate coupés and cabriolets producing less power were sold with high-speed touring in mind; these were bodied by Touring, Stabilimenti Farina, Vignale, Bertone, Ghia and, starting in 1952, Pinin Farina.

In general, those cars carrying even-numbered chassis plates were built for competition and those with odd numbers for road use. But it was the customer who determined the actual use, often dual-purpose. For example, Vignale produced a range of open bodywork on even- and odd-numbered chassis that varied from stark competition spyders through moderately appointed two-seaters to tall, fully-civilized cabriolets. Adding to the confusion is the fact that many early competition cars were rebodied for road use after brief racing careers. In recent years a less satisfactory trend has emerged—rebuilding GT chassis with pseudo-competition body-work. Even worse are the Ferrari 'replicas' built over the chassis of other makers.

But the conversion of a Ferrari berlinetta into its own spyder equivalent, or a coupé into a cabriolet, is certainly a valid exercise when done well. With very few exceptions all the new Ferraris for the past 30 years have been designed by Pinin Farina (Pininfarina, as the firm has been called since 1959), and the chassis are deserving of more exotic variations, such as were common during Ferrari's first ten years of production. But Turin is no longer the centre for panel beating. The United States, England and Germany are now the main locations for exotic-car artisans, whose work may in time earn the respect enjoyed by the 'true' Italian *carrozziere* of old.

Originally trained as an automobile body designer, and having participated in the conversion of a 365GTC/4 coupé into a cabriolet, I naturally entertain this wider view of custom coachwork, all the while remaining in awe of the master craftsmen of Turin and Milan. To me there is nothing more exciting than a spyder, nor more elegant than a cabriolet, and I eagerly await the open Ferraris of the future, whether they are Pininfarina designs built at the Scaglietti plant in Modena or one-offs and limited-series variations produced by Ferrari specialists around the world.

Early custom-bodied cabriolets

The first Ferrari type designed as a road car was the 166 Inter, a tamer single-carburettor version of the racing 2-litre V12, and the first cabriolet in the series was O11 S, built by Stabilimenti Farina.

Located in Turin, as were the majority of Italian coach-builders (to be near Fiat), Stabilimenti Industriali Farina SA was one of the oldest, dating from 1905. Managed by Giovanni Farina, the older brother of the more celebrated Pinin, the firm was noted for a sober line, handsome yet seldom innovative. Of the nine Ferraris it clothed from 1948 to 1952, five were 166 Inter coupés, three 166 Inter cabriolets, and the last one a 212 Export coupé. All but one of these shared the same basic form, 'borrowed' from the famous Pinin Farina Cisitalia coupé and even seen on the French Simca 8 Sport, built later by Facel. A small, tight form with either a fastback roof or a notch-back cabriolet top, the Cisitalia design existed in a number of full-size wood patterns over which the panels were beaten. The patterns were trundled back and forth between the two brothers' shops as the need arose, and were even made available to Vignale when that *carrozzeria* constructed several Cisitalia cabriolets. The proportions changed slightly to suit the different chassis dimensions, but the form remained easily recognizable.

With a slightly higher, wedge-shaped hood (made necessary by the 166 engine's carburettor, in the centre

Right *The first Ferrari cabriolet was 011 S, a 166 Inter with Stabilimenti Farina bodywork resembling that of the famous Pinin Farina Cisitalia*

Below *The basic Cisitalia style appeared on other cabriolets, such as the Vignale-built 202 and the Simca 8 Sport (here) built in France by Facel*

of the vee), the Ferrari version was not quite as successful as that of the Cisitalia, but it was more handsome than the even higher Inter coupés built by Touring and Ghia during the same period.

First shown at the Geneva Salon in 1949, O11 S was the simplest and most attractive of the Stabilimenti Farina cabriolets. Originally painted a light colour (probably sky blue) with tan upholstery and top, it was the first Ferrari purchased by the Italian film director Roberto Rossellini. The grille had five horizontal bars, the wheels were Cabo (Carlo Borrani) knock-off disc type with chromium hubcaps, and the rear wheel arches were round.

The second Stabilimenti Farina cabriolet, built in January 1950, was painted ivory, with blue interior and top. This car, 033 S, had several detail variations which in the writer's opinion made it less attractive: a hood scoop, an 'egg-crate' grille texture cut out at the lower corners for auxilliary driving lights, rear fender contours overlappping the doors, and flattened rear wheel arches. On the other hand, its bumpers, painted body colour and lacking overriders, were better looking.

The firm's third cabriolet, 0063 S, had a completely different body of distinctly more aggressive character. The grille, more typical of Ferrari design, was angled back as on the Grand Prix cars of the period; the front fenders continued straight back to the tail; the windshield was of one piece, slightly curved; and the wheels were Borrani wire knock-offs. Altogether it was a powerful-looking car. While its height was probably not significantly less (if at all) than that of the Cisitalia-derived designs, it had a much more low-slung look, accentuated by the horizontal slots behind the front wheel arches and the chromium rub strips on the flanks at wheel-centre height. Shown at Paris in October 1950 and at Geneva the following March, it appears to have been painted black. Although unique on a Ferrari, the body is similar to one later mounted on a Talbot Lago. Despite the fine impression it made, this effort by

11

The second Stabilimenti Farina cabriolet was 033 S, generally similar to the first but with less successful detailing

A completely different form with straight-through fenders was built by Stabilimenti Farina on 166 Inter chassis 0063 S

Stabilimenti Farina did not prevent the company from going out of business in 1953, after making only one more Ferrari, 0107 E, on a 212 Export chassis. By this time Vignale was doing the majority of the Ferrari sports car bodywork, and Pinin Farina would soon enter the picture.

Alfredo Vignale, whose methods involved metal shaping *without* the use of patterns, employed the very talented designer Giovanni Michelotti, responsible for the dominant Ferrari character through the early 1950s. His sketches were exaggerated but he had an unerring sense of the final form, nearly always taut and clean. The earliest Vignale Ferraris had absolute simplicity, but as competition from Pinin Farina increased (ultimately more commercial in impact than stylistic), Michelotti added more decoration to his designs, with un-satisfactory results. In all, Vignale constructed some 22 Ferrari cabriolets and spyders primarily as road cars, in addition to many purely competition types.

In differentiating between Ferrari road and com-petition types, the general rule was that the former carried odd chassis numbers and the latter even. But the only rule at Maranello, especially during the first ten years, was that variety prevailed: some odd-numbered cars were raced by their owners and some even-numbered high-performance chassis were covered with bodywork meant for daily use on the road. In between these were competition types with *lusso* (de luxe) finish and trim. The first cabriolets and spyders built by Vignale—eight even-numbered 212 Exports—emphasized this dual nature. Of the eight, three were low-slung spyders with abbreviated windshields and five were of the true cabriolet style, with taller windshields and side glass.

Although mentioned for the purpose of perspective, the three spyders almost fall outside the province of this book. Lacking tops and side windows, they nevertheless had *lusso* finish and were clearly built for road use. They were the Vignale equivalent of the Touring barchetta style, some of which were also bought for daily transport rather than racing. In any case, they were among Michelotti's best designs, and thus among the most attractive Ferraris of all time.

The five Vignale 212 Export cabriolets were well pro-portioned but suffered a bit from over-ornamentation, specifically the slotted side strips which ran from the front wheel arches to just behind the doors, then angling upward to the windowsill line. Several of them had complicated grille structures with a vertical centre bar projecting forward from a trim strip down the middle of the hood, but at least one example had the traditional 'egg-crate' design, more simple and more appropriate.

Right and far right *Vignale
built several spyders on 212
Export chassis, with lines
and purpose comparable to
the Touring-built barchetta
series*

The same general cabriolet style (but always with individual variations) continued on six even-numbered 212 Inters, but the 13 in. longer wheelbase (2600 mm on the Inter compared with 2250 on the Export) made for a larger car.

Again for the sake of perspective, the Vignale 225 S spyders must be mentioned. Although these were built mainly for Ferrari's racing clients in 1952, they were very handsome cars—perhaps the zenith of the Vignale style—and several were finished in road trim. (The same can be said for the Vignale 340 America spyders included in Chapter Two.) Fourteen 225 and four 340 spyders were built with this clean, elegant form.

The last Vignale cabriolet was definitely a road car.

True Vignale cabriolets were constructed on the higher 212 Inter chassis, with minor variations in the grilles and other details

A later Vignale style, also used on several coupés, appeared on 0353 EU/Al, begun as a 250 Europa but completed with a 375 engine

Originally begun as a 3-litre 250 Europa with the serial 0353 EU, it was completed in 1954 as a 4.5-litre 375 America with the suffix changed to AL. The longer wheelbase (2800 mm, no less than 110.2 in.) gave it a nice sweep of fender from headlight to rear deck but again it was detailing which spoiled its effect, particularly the reverse-pillar wraparound windshield and the side venting with the lower edges of the surrounding trim continuing through the doors to the rear wheel arches. The grille, recessed within a projecting surround as on the 500 F2 racing cars of the period, was certainly impressive.

Carrozzeria Bertone SA designed only a few Ferraris (discounting the 308GT4, which was built in quantity by Scaglietti). The first and only cabriolet was a 166 Inter of which the serial is unknown but probably one of five unaccounted numbers between 035 S and 0077 S. This was an extremely clean and simple design with the 'standard' Ferrari grille mounted upright, leaning neither forward nor back. There was no attempt to create a rakish line by any artificial surfaces (the only decoration was the oval air outlet on each flank) but the apparent height of the sides was reduced by a horizontal crease about a third of the way up from the rocker panel. Painted a medium blue with tan top and upholstery, the Bertone cabriolet was no less appealing for its 'boulevard' character.

Carrozzeria Ghia SpA, which built a number of Ferrari coupés and berlinettas, produced only two cabriolets, both on 212 Inter chassis. Of essentially the same design, with the exception of colour and minor details, they might best be described as ungainly. Wide flanks and low bumpers gave them a heavy look, while the scoops above the grilles and the partially covered rear wheels were annoying features. The first one, 0191 EL, appeared at the Turin Salon in November 1951, probably painted white; the second, 0233 E, was built in 1952 and carried a dark colour.

In retrospect it is surprising how long it took for

Carrozzeria Pinin Farina SpA and Ferrari to get together. Today they are considered inseparable partners in the creation of exotic high-performance automobiles, but for the first five years of Ferrari's existence, 1947–51, there was an emphasis on competition machinery that was of little interest to the coach-builder. And Ferrari was being well served in that area by Vignale. By the early 1950s Battista (Pinin) Farina had clothed almost every significant make except Ferrari with his designs. His longest association was with Lancia for whom he had been building elegant and innovative bodywork since before World War 2, but it was the creation of the Cisitalia coupé in 1947 that made his name famous throughout the world. Until 1959 he used the name Pinin Farina but his company and legal names were then changed to Pininfarina, uniting his nickname and family name to create a new dynasty. Whether this was by affectation, arrogance or simply good business sense, the name Pininfarina is now universally accepted. In this book the older form Pinin Farina is used for those cars built through to 1958.

The first Pinin Farina Ferrari was a right-hand drive cabriolet on a 212 Inter chassis, built in 1952 for a Swiss customer. Unfortunately its serial number is not known for certain, although it may have been either 0147 E (since rebodied as a spyder by Scaglietti) or 0177 E. It was an extremely sober and elegant design with a long straight fender line and a perfectly proportioned cabriolet top. In order to keep the grille low, in its best position below the tops of the headlights, a higher hood line was subtly disguised by a scoop at its leading edge. The only jarring detail was the second, smaller scoop near the rear of the hood. The body was painted dark blue, the interior was brown leather, and the top was a darker brown fabric.

A second, nearly identical Pinin Farina 212 cabriolet, 0235 EU, can be considered the better looking of the two in that it dispensed with the smaller hood scoop. Painted a light metallic blue, this left-hand drive car was shown

The only Bertone cabriolet on a Ferrari chassis was this 166 Inter. Though simple, its lines were very harmonious and pleasing

Ghia made two cabriolets on 212 Inter chasis, nearly identical except for colour and neither one particularly attractive

at the Paris Salon in October 1952. It actually raced at the Nürburgring the following year, entered by the owner Rossellini, and placed 9th against faster but less handsome machinery. When first brought into the United States it was one of the few Ferraris to mount white-sidewall tyres, if only temporarily.

A similar design was built on the longer 250 Europa chassis in late 1953. Carrying the serial 0311 EU and making its debut at the New York Auto Show in

January 1954, it had a more projecting nose and an angled grille (to balance the extra length within the wheelbase). With no hood scoop at all, it had one of the longest unbroken hoodlines of any 3-litre Ferrari. Although it shared many features with two 342 Americas designed by Pinin Farina (discussed in Chapter Two), it was the only 250 Europa cabriolet built.

Carrozzeria Touring, often referred to as Touring Superleggera because of the superlight method of construction it employed, was one of the few coach-builders to be located in Milan (near its main client Alfa Romeo) rather than Turin. Run by Felice Bianchi Anderloni until his death in 1948, Touring was then

The first Pinin Farina Ferrari was this sober, dark blue 212 Inter. The lines were clean and the proportions of the top were excellent

The second Pinin Farina cabriolet, 212 Inter 0235 EU, was nearly identical except for the omission of the scoop at the rear of the hood

taken over by his son Carlo Felice, who had been responsible for most of the design direction since 1945. Touring was one of the first collaborators with Ferrari, producing a series of competition spyders known as barchettas (literally 'little boats', because the smooth upper surfaces, pierced only by the open cockpits, resembled those of contemporary speedboats). Although a few of the barchettas were purchased for road use (there are two carrying odd chassis numbers), they generally lacked tops and do not fit within the confines of this book. A possible exception is a long-wheelbase barchetta, 0253 EU, built on a 212 Inter chassis to the order of the Ford Motor Company in Dearborn. An awkward design because of the extra 350 mm of wheelbase, it was the last road Ferrari built by Touring.

The honour of making the first 250GT cabriolet fell to Carrozzeria Boano. Although its director, Mario Boano, was prominent among Italian *carrozziere*, having worked with Stabilimenti Farina, Pinin Farina and Ghia, the firm bearing his name was in existence for only four years, from 1954 to 1957, when it was dissolved so that he might set up the Centro Stile for Fiat. During this short period Boano concentrated on building the 250GT coupé design created by Pinin Farina, handing it over in turn to Carrozzeria Ellena in 1957, but he also produced a few original designs. One of these was the only 250GT cabriolet *not* to be built by Pinin Farina; shown at the Geneva Salon in 1956, this was 0461 GT, a car of imposing but not entirely successful styling features. The very low grille and high fenders were effective, and

Of the same concept was this 250 Europa cabriolet, chassis 0311 EU

Above and right *Technically the first 250GT cabriolet, 0461 GT was a Boano one-off with a handsome top but ridiculous American-inspired tailfins*

the proportions of the fabric top were superb, but the outward curving tailfins, a concession to American practice of the period, were discordant in the extreme. The low bumpers, with vertical ends, were an interesting feature that worked well in front but only added to the chaos at the rear.

Left *The last barchetta by Touring was this 212 Inter, 0253 EU. Stretching the form over the longer chassis spoiled the barchetta look*

A little known Ferrari was this 212 Inter cabriolet (sorry, drophead coupé) constructed by Abbott in England. Neither typically British nor Italian in character, it was still recognizable as a Ferrari

Early custom-bodied cabriolets

166 Inter	Three Stabilimenti Farina—011 S, 033 S, 0063 S
	One Vignale—051 S (originally a Vignale berlinetta and later rebodied as a cabriolet)
	One Bertone—serial unknown (possibly 035 S, 055 S, 0073 S, 0075 S or 0077 S)
	Also two odd-numbered Touring spyders with competition-type barchetta bodywork—0057 S, 0067 S
212 Export	Eight even-numbered Vignale spyders and cabriolets with varying degrees of road trim—0076 E, 0086 E, 0090 E, 0098 E, 0106 E, 0110 E, 0214 ED
212 Inter	Six Vignale—0117 S (originally built as a 195 Inter), 0125 EL, 0159 EL, 0207 EL, 0209 EL, 0227 EL (renumbered as 0255 EU)
	One Abbott—0165 EL
	Two Pinin Farina—first serial unknown (possibly 0147 E or 0177 E), 0235 EU
	Two Ghia—0191 EL, 0233 E
	One Touring—0253 EU (with stretched barchetta-style bodywork)
225 Export	One Vignale—0273 EU
	Also 14 even-numbered Vignale 225 S spyders, some in road trim—0154 ED, 0160 ED, 0162 ED, 0172 ET, 0176 ED, 0180 ED, 0182 ED, 0186 ED, 0192 ET, 0194 ET, 0198 ET, 0216 ED, 0218 ET, 0220 ED
250 Europa	One Pinin Farina—0311 EU
	One Vignale—0353 EU/AL (completed as a 375 America)
250GT	One Boano—0461 GT

---

45 cars (possibly six to eight other unknown examples)

Cabriolets for the elite

Once Enzo Ferrari accepted the fact that he would have to produce road cars in support of his racing programme, and that many of his customers had no interest whatsoever in campaigning their machines, the time was ripe for truly elegant and exclusive designs for the very wealthy—royalty, movie stars and industrialists among them. By the mid-1950s Ferrari was already producing large-capacity engines for competition and it was natural that they be adapted for street use.

In developing the 4.5-litre, Aurelio Lampredi-designed V12 for Formula 1 Grand Prix racing, Ferrari arrived at an interim capacity of 4.1 litres. In sports car form this engine was known as the 340 America (and later as the 340 Mexico and Mille Miglia). Essentially still intended for competition, the 340 Americas carried even serial numbers and, initially, Touring barchetta bodies. These were followed by several berlinettas and coupés with bodies constructed by Touring, Vignale and Ghia, and then by a series of four Vignale spyders of the same basic style as that used on the contemporary 225 S. The Vignale 340s were very handsomely detailed and can be considered as road cars even though they did not have tops. At any rate, the inclusion of the type in this books is justified on the basis of its traditional nature, as well as for its beautiful lines; the example pictured, 0140 A, is one of the author's all-time favourite Ferraris.

But the first series of Ferraris built specifically for the

Using the lines already presented on the 212 Inter and 250 Europa cabriolets, Pinin Farina built two 342 Americas, 0234 AL and 0248 AL

One of the most beautiful Ferraris of all time was 0140 A, a 340 America spyder built by Vignale in 1952

conspicuously wealthy—as opposed to the sport-oriented—clientèle was the 342 America. This street version of the 340 had the same basic engine, detuned to 200 bhp, on a 2650 mm wheelbase. Fitted with left-hand drive, only six 342s were built, half of them coupés and half cabriolets. The two Pinin Farina cabriolets, 0234 AL and 0248 AL, continued the theme set on the 212s and the 250 Europa by this body-maker, although with longer noses. The two were similar to each other in most respects other than paint; 0248 AL had the forward hood scoop blended into the hood contours, as opposed to the tacked-on look of 0234 AL. (In both cases, one suspects

*An absolute one of a kind
was this imposing Pinin
Farina cabriolet, combining
a fully padded top with
competition-inspired lines.
Built on 375MM chassis 0488
AM, it had a 4.9-litre V12*

that the reason for this feature was to clear the radiator while allowing a generally lower line to the projecting grille.) The other 342 America cabriolet (actually the first of the series, 0232 AL) had Vignale bodywork.

The 342 series was in production for only four months during the winter of 1952–53 before being supplanted by the 375 America, with engine displacement increased from 4.1- to 4.5-litres. Other than 0353 EU, originally a 250 Europa, none of the 375 Americas had cabriolet bodywork, but one unique machine was built on the 375 Mille Miglia chassis. Although the latter was basically for competition, the 375MM cabriolet built for the King of Belgium by Pinin Farina on chassis 0488 AM was an elegant one-of-a-kind, obviously constructed for touring use yet all the more unusual in having the 4.9-litre displacement of the 375 Plus competition spyders! As we shall see, this engine was a step in the direction of the 410 Superamerica series. King Leopold's 0488 AM had a low, wide grille flanked by small bumpers, and the more or less 'standard' Pinin Farina straight fender line of that period was replaced by one that curved gracefully downward, including the window-sill, and then kicked up again over the real wheels. Contrasting with the very sporting contours of the all-black car were the elegantly appointed interior, in light green leather, and the large, fully padded top of black fabric to emphasize the dignity of this very special machine.

When the 410 Superamerica, the first truly elite series of Ferraris, arrived on the scene in 1956, Pinin Farina had all but taken over the clothing of the Ferrari road cars. Yet of the 15 Series I, 8 Series II and 13 (documented) Series III 410s, only one was a cabriolet and it was constructed by Boano. Carrying the serial number 0485 SA and painted white, it was almost identical in all details to the Boano 250GT cabriolet described in Chapter One, except for the additional 200 mm (7.9 in.) of wheelbase, added between the front wheels and the cowl.

Production of the 410 continued into 1959, when it was

replaced by the 400 Superamerica. Whereas the 410 designation had roughly indicated the single-cylinder capacity (actually 413.5 cc) of the 4.9-litre engines, the new 400 label indicated a 4-litre engine (3967 cc). The wheelbases of the 400, originally 2420 mm and increased to 2600 mm in 1962, were shorter than on the 410s and gave the new series a heftier, more compact look, especially the Pininfarina (new spelling) aerodynamic

First exhibited as a 400 Superamerica prototype by Pininfarina, this cabriolet may be the 250GT Cabriolet Speciale, 1737 GT, shown in Chapter Three with bumpers and hardtop

Left *Nearly identical to its 250GT exercise (Chapter One), this white Boano cabriolet, 0485 SA, used a 410 Superamerica chassis*

Below *Although only a few 400 Superamerica cabriolets were built, and each differed in detail, this rear three-quarter view shows the more or less standard configuration*

Shown after its restoration in Modena in 1976, this 400 Superamerica, 3309 SA, has the hardtop and the faired-in headlight covers

A nearly identical 400 Superamerica with uncovered headlights and lacking the trim strips along the flanks

coupés based on the Superfast show car. But there were also six Pininfarina cabriolets on the 2420 mm wheelbase Series I and four more on the longer Series II; these might be described as having the look of Pininfarina's 250GT Cabriolets (see Chapter Three) but with the cockpits further forward. Some had headlights faired in by plastic covers, others had normal uncovered lights with chromium bezels, and most of them had removable hardtops which were well integrated when in place. All were characterized by very low and wide grilles, horizontal creases running from the front to the rear wheel arches, and forward-leaning taillight housings.

Two Scaglietti spyder bodies were made on the short 400 Superamerica chassis. One, number 2311 SA, is a well documented right-hand drive car built for Michel Paul-Cavallier; the other is a less well-known example with left-hand drive. Both had the lines of Scaglietti's last series of short-wheelbase Spyder Californias, (see Chapter Four) which differed by only 20 mm (0.8 in.) from the 400 SA.

When the 400 series ended in 1964 it was replaced by the 5-litre 500 Superfast, but no cabriolet bodies were built on these chassis. In 1966 an entirely new model, exclusively of cabriolet design, was made available to Ferraris' special clients. Known as the 365 California, it had a 4.4-litre V12 mounted in a 2650 mm chassis. A long, low hood and a fairly long tail made this an impressive form, especially with the top down. The headlights were faired in (another pair of pop-up driving lights was recessed into the nose) and horizontal scoops were set

Exhibited at Paris as a 400 Superamerica, this Scaglietti spyder had bodywork indistinguishable from the 250GT Spyder California style

*The first 365 California
cabriolet, 8347, made its debut
at the 1966 Geneva Show.
Note the Dino-style side
scoops and the retractable
driving lights on the nose*

into the doors in a manner similar to the Dinos of the period and which continues on the 308GTB/GTS to this day. The tail had an angular, almost chiselled design not unlike Pininfarina's Fiat 124 Spider. Only 14 365 Californias were built during 1966–67. Two were right-hand drive models but most of the others found customers in the United States.

The 365 California may be described as the last Ferrari cabriolet for elite clientèle. No factory cabriolets were built on the 365GT 2+2, 365GT4 2+2 nor 400GT/A/i series, even though several conversions (mainly on the latter chassis) were done later and are discussed in Chapter Six.

Cabriolets for the elite

342 America	One Vignale—0232 AL Two Pinin Farina—0234 AL, 0248 AL (completed as a 375 America) Also four Vignale 340 America spyders with some degree of road trim—0138 A, 0140 A, 0204 A, 0238 A
375 Mille Miglia	One Pinin Farina—0488 AM (with 375 Plus engine)
410 Superamerica	One Boano—0485 SA

400 Superamerica
   (Series I)
	Six Pininfarina—1611 SA, 1885 SA, 1945 SA, 2331 SA, 2407 SA,
	   3309 SA
	Two Scaglietti—2311 SA, other serial unknown

(Series II)	Four Pininfarina—4241 SA, 4423 SA, 4781 SA, 5093 SA
365 California	14 Pininfarina—08347, 09127, 09447, 09615, 09631, 09801, 09849, 09889, 09935, 09985, 10077, 10155, 10327, 10369

35 cars

Production cabriolets from Pininfarina

One of the most famous of all types of Ferrari was the 250GT. In fact, it was a series of cars that included coupés, cabriolets, berlinettas, spyders and even 2+2s, with different wheelbase lengths. Even though the common factor in the series, which lasted from 1954–64, was the 3-litre V12 engine, even this differed in specification and power output according to the purpose of the car.

There were several predecessors of the Pinin Farina/Pininfarina cabriolets which form the basis of this chapter, including the Pinin Farina 250 Europa cabriolet (0311 EU) and Boano 250GT cabriolet (0461 GT) presented in Chapter One. But the first real 250GT cabriolet was the prototype 0655 GT, built by Pinin Farina in 1957 and shown at Geneva that year. Originally painted red, it was later refinished in dark green for Peter Collins and received such characteristically British equipment as Dunlop disc brakes and alloy wheels. The cut-down door on the driver's side (the left!) was also of English roadster inspiration. Other details unique to 0655 GT were the long hood scoop, the more pointed headlight fairings, the unframed top of the windshield, and the rear bumper extensions on the flanks.

A typical prototype, 0663 GT, followed. This had a racing windscreen, headrest and tonneau, but the proportions were otherwise similar to the Collins car.

Then came two prototypes which can be regarded as the true forerunners of the production series; carrying the numbers 0705 GT and 0709 GT, they were almost identical except for the air outlets on the flanks of the former and the vent windows on the doors of the latter. Neither detail was normal for the production series of 36 250GT cabriolets which began with 0729 GT late in 1957 and ended with 1475 GT in 1959. Most of the Series I cabriolets had the small bumpers below each headlight but, beginning with 0981 GT in late 1958, a full-width front bumper was mounted below the grille.

The prototype for the Series II cars was 1213 GT, built early in 1959 (by which time the body-maker's name was spelt Pininfarina). Of generally similar lines, it had revised rear fenders and uncovered headlights, which took away some of the character of the original series even if more practical for regular use. Then began a long run (by Ferrari standards of that time) of 209 Series II cabriolets, beginning with 1537 GT and ending with 3807 GT in 1962. With the revised headlights and rear fenders,

Far left and below The first prototype for the long series of 250GT cabriolets by Pinin Farina was this spyder, 0655 GT, with cut-down driver's door. Originally painted red, it was later refinished in dark green for Peter Collins and eventually got disc brakes and alloy disc wheels

Below Called the 250GT Spyder Competizione, this second Pinin Farina prototype, 0663 GT, had a racing type windshield and headrest

The third 250GT prototype, 0705 GT, was near to production form except for the large air outlets on the flanks

they very much resembled the 250GT coupés of the period, especially when fitted (very neatly) with the optional body-coloured hardtop. Most of the series had hood scoops, but there were several without. One car, 1737 GT, was built to special order in 1960 with bodywork almost identical to the 400 Superamerica cabriolet. It is very likely that the bumperless '400 SA' shown in Chapter Two was 1737 GT with the 3-litre engine, standing in as the prototype for the 4-litre series.

Just as Ferrari constantly increased the engine capacity of his competition sports cars during the 1960s, he also introduced mildly tuned versions of these larger units into the production cars. In 1964 came the 275GTS, a series of 203 cars with much more sedate appearance despite the improved performance of the 3.3-litre engine. While the 250GTs, with their long hoods and small cockpits, had been called cabriolets, the S of the 275GTS series stood for spyder, even though the newer type had a shorter hood and roomier cockpit. Although not often seen, a hardtop was again an option.

The fourth prototype, 0709 GT, was standard in all details except for the vent windows, not used on production cabriolets

CHAPTER THREE

Two production 250GT cabriolets, 0735 GT and 0737 GT, the latter having the non-standard fender outlets seen on 0705 GT

Early and late production cabriolets, showing the original small bumpers (0801 GT) and the later full-width type (0981 GT)

The Series II cabriolet, with more sober lines and uncovered headlamps, made its debut at the Paris Salon in 1959. Note the full instrumentation and tall gearshift lever

*This Series II cabriolet lacked
a hood scoop but was
otherwise standard*

Another view of a Series II cabriolet with the hardtop

Designated 250GT Cabriolet Speciale, 1737 GT was a one-off with 400 Superamerica-style bodywork. It may have been the same car originally exhibited as a 400 (see Chapter Two) with the bumpers and hardtop added

One hundred 330GTS spyders were built with the still larger 4-litre V12, beginning in 1966. In addition to the greater power the 330GTS had a longer, lower, more aggressive nose, with two horizontal bumper halves, and alloy wheels (although the Borrani wire wheels were still an option). With the larger capacity it was possible to achieve better performance at reduced engine speeds,

An American-owned 250GT Series II photographed in the Nevada desert in 1972

making the car more tractable, and new engine/transmission mounts made the cars much quieter than the 275.

Using identical bodywork but a further increase in capacity to 4.4 litres, the 365GTS had an output of 320 bhp at 6600 rpm, compared with the 240 bhp at 7000 rpm of the original 250GT cabriolets. The only significant

61

Although more sedate in appearance than the 250GT cabriolet, the 275GTS introduced in 1964 received the spyder designation

This 275GTS was tested by Road & Track magazine in 1966; it reached 60 mph from rest in 7.2 seconds and a maximum of 145 mph in 5th gear

external feature that distinguished the 365GTS from the earlier series was the removal of the air outlets from the flanks, replaced by outlets at the back of the engine lid; in fact, Ferrari never published a photo of a true 365GTS, using instead an airbrushed photo of the 330GTS for its press release. In any case, only 20 of the larger cars were built before production ended in 1969. These represented the last soft-top Ferraris to be built by Pininfarina until the introduction of the Mondial Cabriolet Quattrovalvole in 1983. As we shall see in Chapter Four, the production of the most sporting road Ferraris was turned over to Scaglietti in Modena (even though the designs were still by the Pininfarina studio in Turin.)

Superb 212 Export Vignale cabriolet taken in 1974. From this distance its well-balanced if slightly crouching-ready-to-spring stance is obvious

Above *Magnificent 400SA with the hood down. It's a large car by contemporary standards – much longer than the 308GT4 next to it*

Above right *Historic racing at Monterey in 1982 – long wheelbase (LWB) 250GT spyder California*

Right *Cockpit of a Pinin Farina 375MM cabriolet chassis number 0488*

250 granturismo cabriolet

Left *Straight from the lovely factory colour brochure of the series 1 250GT cabriolet. The car is long if nothing else*

Above left *Somewhat later, the same profile, this time for the 275GTS, also from the factory brochure*

Above *A Pininfarina promotional shot of the 330GTS – a not unhandsome profile*

Top left *Shot by author Jonathan Thompson, this is an injection 308GTS with the roof panel removed*

Bottom left *The Michelotti-bodied 365GTB/4-S NART. Its side profile could be confused for that of a well-known American built fibreglass sportscar . . .*

Right *Mondial cabriolet complete with 4-valve engine taken in America, not Italy*

Top *Daytona convertible
conversions have proven to be
popular. This one is such a
car – not one of the rare
factory-built cars*

Above *Another conversion,
this time rarer because it's on
the 365GTC/4 chassis.
Handsome for a big car*

*The 1965 version of the
275GTS had revised air
outlets on the front fenders
and a hardtop was an
optional item*

With the larger 4-litre V12, the 330GTS had a longer nose and alloy disc wheels

Then during the 1970s the convertible, or drophead, went into a worldwide decline; Ferrari continued to make open cars, but these were of the Targa style, with rollbars and rear windows.

A special 330GTS constructed in 1969 by William Harrah emphasized the new trend. Converted into a Targa, it had a large polished rollbar and a huge rear window that required the rear deck lid to be shortened. While the Harrah Targa probably had improved comfort for high-speed cruising, it detracted from the open-air spirit of the original.

Above *William Harrah
converted one 330GTS (10913)
into Targa configuration*

Below *This factory photo of
the 365GTS was actually an
airbrush retouching of a
330GTS. Air outlets were
moved to the top of the hood*

Also tested by Road & Track, *the 330GTS was marginally faster (0–60 in 6.9 seconds, 146 mph) than its predecessor. Wire wheels were still an option*

With the hindsight of 1984, it is ironic that it was lack of demand that was the main factor in the demise of the soft-top convertible Ferrari at the end of the 1960s. When they were current, the 250GT and the 275/330/365GTS cabriolets and spyders were almost taken for granted, not enjoying the respect that was afforded the most sporting 250GT berlinetta and spyder California, and later the four-camshaft 275GTB/4 and 365GTB/4 Daytona. Today their open-air charm—and relative rarity—make them among the most desired of Ferraris, collectors' items all. Of the approximately 6000 road Ferraris built between 1957 and 1969, only 573 were cabriolets and spyders—fewer than ten per cent.

Production cabriolets from Pininfarina

250GT	Four prototypes—0655 GT, 0663 GT (spyder), 0705 GT, 0709 GT
(Series I)	36—0729 GT, 0735 GT, 0737 GT, 0759 GT, 0775 GT, 0777 GT, 0779 GT, 0783 GT, 0789 GT, 0791 GT, 0795 GT, 0799 GT, 0801 GT, 0809 GT, 0811 GT, 0813 GT, 0829 GT, 0845 GT, 0849 GT, 0873 GT, 0913 GT, 0915 GT, 0917 GT, 0921 GT, 0961 GT, 0963 GT, 0979 GT, 0981 GT, 1075 GT, 1079 GT, 1179 GT, 1181 GT, 1193 GT, 1211 GT, 1439 GT, 1475 GT
(Series II)	One prototype—1213 GT 209—beginning 1537 GT, ending 3807 GT
275GTS	203—beginning 6001, ending 8653
330GTS	100—beginning 8899, ending 11363
365GTS	20—beginning 12163, ending 12493

573 cars

Scaglietti V12 spyders

Carrozzeria Scaglietti of Modena became the principal builder of competition bodywork for Ferrari in the mid-1950s. With such famous designs as the 750 Monza, his work gave the racing machinery a distinctively aggressive appearance, with exciting and often flamboyant compound curves. It was only natural that when Ferrari began a series of higher-performance road cars, he would choose Scaglietti to build the bodies. Scaglietti's shop was close to Maranello and his production methods were more suited to small runs than those of Pinin Farina, ever more industrial in its nature.

The first 'production' cars by Scaglietti were the long-wheelbase 250GT berlinettas and spyder Californias. Both were catalogued models but they were intended mainly for competitive enthusiasts, with an increased power output of 280 bhp from the 3-litre V12. The basic design of the spyder California was still by Pinin Farina and generally similar to the 250GT cabriolet, but it had a more rakish line, especially in front. The initial California was 0769 GT, constructed at the end of 1957. The chassis, at 2600 mm, was long for a car intended for racing, but this made it stable at very high speeds (as at Le Mans) and the use of alloy rather than steel for the doors and deck lids saved about 200 lb compared with the cabriolets. Interiors were less fully trimmed than on the cabriolets, but still not stark by any means. The fabric tops had an extremely rakish and attractive line when

A 250GT spyder California under construction at Maranello in 1958

erect. Some examples had uncovered rather than faired-in headlights.

Although not campaigned quite as extensively as its berlinetta counterpart, the spyder California had a significant and successful competition career, especially at Le Mans and Sebring. The highest overall placing in an international event was the 5th place at Le Mans by the spyder California (1451 GT) of Fernand Tavano and Bob Grossman in 1959; almost as impressive was the 9th overall and GT class win by Richie Ginther and Howard Hively at Sebring the same year.

But greater manoeuvrability and a reduction in weight were desirable. After 50 of the long-wheelbase Californias had been built, the later examples having outside-plug engines and disc brakes, a new chassis made its appearance at the Geneva Salon in 1960. The wheelbase was reduced 200 mm to 2400 (94.4 in.) and the bodywork, while continuing the established line, had a slightly more rounded, hefty character. The carburettor air scoop was partially recessed into the hood. As on the 250GT cabriolets, a hardtop (more compact but less well integrated) was offered on the California. In all, 75 of the short-wheelbase Californias were made, beginning with 1795 GT in 1960 and ending with 4137 GT in 1962. They

The lines of the spyder California were essentially derived from those of the 250GT berlinetta, also built by Scaglietti

This factory photo of the 1958 spyder California show its general similarity to the 250GT cabriolet. The side view emphasizes the long wheelbase of the first series

are among the most prized of road Ferraris today.

A period of five years would elapse before Scaglietti would again build spyders, and then only a special run of ten for Luigi Chinetti's North American Racing Team. Built on modified four-camshaft 275GTB/4 chassis in 1967, they were designated 275GTB/4-S NART. The conversion was straightforward but attractive, making the 3.3-litre, 300 bhp car one of the most exhilarating in the world to drive. The fabric top was small but neatly

done, and the lower rear deck retained the spoiler of its berlinetta origins. Because the original 275GTB/4-S NARTs were converted directly from GTB bodies (meaning that the tops were cut off of existing berlinetta shells), it has been possible for shops to make almost identical spyder replicas from GTBs by doing the same today. They do not have the same collector value as the known Scaglietti conversions, but in most cases the techniques are as good and in some cases superior (particularly with regard to the elimination of rust).

Toward the end of the first series of long-wheelbase spyder Californias, in 1959, the headlights were changed to the uncovered type

Above *A beautifully prepared spyder California, 1451 GT, as it exists today, owned by Jon Masterson*

Right *The spyder California also looked good with its top erect*

Far right *Spyder California 1451 GT at Le Mans in 1959, when it placed 5th overall in the hands of Fernand Tavano and Bob Grossman*

Above *A short-wheelbase spyder California at Sebring in 1960. The bumpers have been removed and a rollbar added*

Right *Complete with hardtop, this short-wheelbase spyder California takes the start in the 1961 Eberbach hillclimb in Germany*

When the famous 365GTB/4 Daytona appeared at Paris in 1968, it was one of the most successful Pininfarina designs ever, with a low, wide nose, a beautifully integrated roof line, and non-existant rear fenders. Again there was a Scaglietti spyder conversion of this model, first appearing at the Frankfurt Show the following year. In the writer's opinion, this is one of the most beautiful Ferraris of all time, especially the proportions of the fabric top. This was a regular (though limited-production) Ferrari model, rather than a NART special, with 136 examples built in Modena, the serial numbers beginning with 12851 and ending with 17073 in 1973. Exactly the same thing has happened to Daytonas in recent years as with the 275GTBs: various specialist shops have made the spyder conversions with the same desirable but unpedigreed results. More Daytona than

Above *Built in limited
numbers for Luigi Chinetti,
the 275GTB/4-S NART was a
Scaglietti spyder conversion
of the 275GTB berlinetta. It
makes an interesting
comparison with the 365
California beside it*

Right *This 275GTB/4-S
NART was tested by* Road &
Track *at Lime Rock,
Connecticut in 1967. It got to
60 mph in 6.7 seconds and
had a top speed of 155 mph*

275GTB conversions have been made because of the larger number of existing berlinettas.

Although not really an open car, a special Pininfarina 365GTB/4 coupé shown at Paris in 1969, should be mentioned here because it resembled the spyder style with a fixed hardtop added.

By the mid-1970s Scaglietti had become the body-

Scaglietti introduced a spyder variation of the 365GTB/4 Daytona at Frankfurt in 1969. Called the 365GTS/4, 136 examples were built

maker for all the high-performance berlinetta and spyder Ferraris (today the Modena facility is an official wholly-owned part of the Ferrari complex). Construction methods, while far from mass production by world standards, had changed dramatically from the one-car-at-time procedure that Scaglietti had used for the competition cars in the 1950s. As will be seen in Chapter Five, the Dino and 308 spyders built by Scaglietti would overshadow the production of bodies by Pininfarina, the Turin firm becoming Ferrari's design studio (as well as for other companies) and only producing bodies in limited numbers for such chassis as the 365GTC/4, 365GT4 2+2 and 400GT/A/i, all elite cars of the highest class.

Scaglietti V12 spyders

250GT California
  (Long-wheelbase)   50—beginning 0769 GT, ending 1715 GT
  (Short-wheelbase)   75—beginning 1795 GT, ending 4137 GT

275GTB/4-S NART   Ten—09437, 09751, 10139, 10219, 10249, 10453, 10691, 10709, 10749, 11057
  Also perhaps as many as 20 conversions from 275GTB and GTB/4 berlinettas

365GTS/4 Daytona   136—beginning 12851, ending 17073
  Also perhaps as many as 30 conversions from 365GTB/4 Daytona berlinettas

---

271 original cars

Dino and 308 spyders and cabriolets

Now we come to two series of Ferraris which, for sheer numbers, overshadow all the open cars that had been built before: the Dino 246GTS, 308GTS and Mondial Cabriolets. Some Ferrari 'purists' may argue that these are not true Ferraris (indeed the 246GTS was built with the Dino nameplate) because of their V6 and V8 engines. But the V12, while long the most characteristic of Ferrari powerplants, has only been one of the many configurations used by the firm, in racing as well as for road cars.

The main concern of this book is bodywork, and the significance of the 246GTS and 308GTS models is that they are Targas, with removable roof panels rather than folding fabric tops. Production of the 206GT berlinetta began early in 1969, followed by the larger 2.4-litre version at the end of the year. The spyder version, the 246GTS, was introduced at the Geneva Salon in the spring of 1972; the lines were essentially the same as for the berlinetta but three slots replaced the quarter window on each sail panel and the removable roof was black rather than body colour. Along with the success of the basic model, the spyder version enjoyed a significant run—1180 examples, beginning with (Dino) serial 02132 and ending with 08518 in 1974.

The 308 series also began as a Dino model, although the GT4 coupés (a Bertone design) later became known as Ferraris. One of these chassis (12788), with the

Previous page and right
*Designated 246GTS, the
spyder version of the Dino
coupé was introduced in 1972;
1180 examples of this popular
Targa were made*

wheelbase shortened from 2550 mm to 2450 mm, was
built with a one-of-a-kind Bertone body known as the
Rainbow. Of very angular conception, it had a
disappearing (rather than removable) roof panel that
dropped behind the seats.

When the 308GTB appeared in 1975 it was a pure
Ferrari built on Scaglietti's production line in Modena.
Destined to become the most-produced Ferrari in
history, it was followed by a GTS model in 1977, when it
made its debut at Frankfurt. The same sort of

modifications were made as had been done with the 246GTS, but the sail panels had oblique vanes through which (to the right at least) the driver had some rear-quarter vision. Initially, the 308GTS was seen as an addition to the 308 line, but its overwhelming acceptance (especially in the United States) has caused its production to outstrip the berlinetta version.

Beginning as a carburetted 90-degree V8 with 255 bhp (European version) the 308GTS subsequently received fuel injection (as the 308GTSi in the fall of 1980) and a 4-valve head (as the 308GTSi Quattrovalvole in the winter of 1982). These improvements did not so much increase the power (except in the United States, where it was sorely lacking because of emissions requirements) as improve the flexibility. The changes to the 308GTS bodywork have been slight over its seven-year history, the most notable being in the design of the front airdam, larger bumpers for the United States (as well as a temporary black-underneath paint scheme that emulated the BB512), and a BB-type airfoil on the roof of the latest Quattrovalvole. With production continuing,

Bertone built this special Rainbow with disappearing top on Dino 308GT chassis 12788, its wheelbase shortened from 2550 to 2450 mm

A prototype for the 308GTS, photographed at the entrance to the factory in 1977. The prominent rollbar was not retained, fortunately!

Opposite page *The production 308GTS was introduced in the autumn of 1977. Built by Scaglietti in Modena, it has become the most-produced Ferrari body style of all time*

one can only estimate the number of the 308GTS spyders produced so far, but it is probably close to 6200 as of mid-1984.

Replacing the Bertone-designed 308GT4 coupé was the Mondial 8 by Pininfarina, a rather dumpy 2+2 that has not enjoyed great success on the market (it is more of a sop to responsible, as opposed to seemingly frivolous, road transport than a truly practical four-seater). To enliven its image, and give the Ferrari customer the option of a true fabric-top cabriolet, Pininfarina designed a reasonably handsome variation which came on the market at the end of 1983. Known as the Mondial Cabriolet Quattrovalvole (the numeral '8' was dropped from the designation), it has the increased power of the 4-valve head to boost its performance in objective terms, and the sensation of open-air motoring to raise it

98

subjectively. As the author wrote in his May 1984 road test for *Road & Track* magazine:

'When we first tested the Ferrari Mondial 8 (2½ years ago, in the November 1981 issue) we found it less than fast and more than a little dumpy. Trying to move its 3640 lb, even the excellent 308 engine (still in 2-valve form) was uninspiring. The car had Ferrari's typically good gearbox, brakes and handling, but we wondered who the intended customer really was. Who would choose the Mondial, not even a good 2+2, let alone a real 4-seater, over the quicker, more nimble and rakish 308GTBi or GTSi?

'If you're an affluent open-air driving enthusiast, there's now a pretty good reason: a true folding soft-top version, the first regular production cabriolet from Ferrari since the 330/365 GTS models of—good grief!—the early Seventies. Add the Quattrovalvole (4-valve) cylinder heads and 25 more *cavalli* and you have a Mondial with some spirit. Not the same car at all.

'It's even lighter (though not light) at 3545 lb. Whether Pininfarina saved some weight in converting it from the coupe (the rear glass of which would be a significant amount) or whether our 1981 test coupe was an excessively heavy early production example, this one is nearly 100 lb leaner. It even looks leaner, and Pininfarina has done a good job on the top, both esthetically and functionally. Up, the black fabric top gives the Mondial a rakish line; down, it makes the car festive and inviting. This is the car for the boulevardier, the Monte Carlo or Newport Beach sportsman hard at play.

'We were pretty skeptical about the top, having heard stories of a diabolically difficult mechanism and wondering where, between rear seat and engine, they could have found a place to stow it. It's definitely a 2-man top, but if you read the instruction manual and make sure that one of the crucial bows is held at right angle as the top goes down, it's a piece of cake. It does protrude above the rear deck when down, and with the Mondial's low seating you really must depend on the mirror for rearward vision. What Pininfarina has done is leave part of each rear sail in place; this shape is duplicated by the protective boot, helping to minimize the apparent height of the folded top. Another good touch is the provision of retractable quarter windows, which can be lowered electrically even with the top up. There is a certain amount of drumming from the top driving with it up; this becomes obtrusive at about 85 mph, then surprisingly diminishes and gradually builds up again as the car approaches its maximum speed.

'What kind of use will the Mondial Cabriolet get? We still don't see it as a 4-seater—even children aren't well accommodated in the back—but as a 2-seater with very occasional short-run rear seating, such as a blast from cabaña to cafe on a sunny day with the top down. The interior is still not especially luxurious for a $65,000-plus car, nor particularly well arranged. To get the seating package within the

Opposite page *The rear aspect of the 1979 US version of the 308GTS. In addition to the side marker lights, the larger bumpers were a major exterior difference from the European type*

The 1982 308 GTSi had fuel injection. The steering wheel, console and seats, differ from the 1979 model

wheelbase (quite a bit of which is used by the engine, even though transverse), the front seats have been shoved forward, very near to the large front wheelhouses, giving the driver and front passenger a shoehorned feeling that is made worse by the low cushion height, which reduces the view all around. If you're driving fast, only looking down the road, it's not a problem, but maneuvering in dense traffic requires a less than graceful amount of neck craning.

'Fortunately, all the controls are where they should be; the steering wheel rim is of just the right thickness and when you drop your right hand, that very positive shift lever is right there. Not so good is the view of the instruments; for some drivers the tachometer is obscured by the wheel. The seats and door panels are covered in simple but high-quality tan leather, the lighter color making the interior design less forbidding than on previous Mondials in black. We were also pleased to see that the formerly protruding mesh speakers (which could scrape the knuckles of the left hand when the brake lever was being used) have been replaced by nicely integrated grilles in the door panels. But the ventilation system is mediocre for such an expensive car; the center vents put out a fair volume of air but the lack of side vents limits the effectiveness on a really hot day. But then, the top ought to be down, right?

'The Quattrovalvole, as we said in our more recent 308GTBi test, is a superb engine, growly and eager, giving out a wonderful howl at its maximum of 7700 rpm. The Mondial gearing has been changed to suit the Quattrovalvole's characteristics; the final drive is numerically higher (4.06:2 versus 3.71), 1st and 5th are slightly lower, and the middle three ratios remain the same, the result being moderately shorter gearing throughout. The 4-valve engine gives vastly improved performance off the line, as Americans are wont to enjoy, much stronger acceleration all the way up, and an increase in top speed, now 138 mph at 6800 rpm in 5th. Cruising for long distances can be unpleasantly loud, more so than with the steel top; the problem is not so much engine noise as structure resonance. Frankly, the top end of the performance spectrum would be better enjoyed in a GTB or GTS, but the Mondial Cabriolet will *feel* just as fast because of its higher sensory inputs.

'Using a positive but not excessively heavy clutch, the Mondial can be eased through the gears in a relaxed manner or driven fiercely for all it's worth. The shifting, within the beautiful, no-nonsense gate, needs to be done with absolute assurance; you can't get it into the

Introduced in 1983, the 308 GTSi Quattrovalvole (4-valve cylinder heads) can be distinguished by its BB-type roof spoiler. This is a US model with the larger bumpers

Ferrari's first cabriolet in over ten years is the Mondial Quattrovalvole, built by Scaglietti to a Pininfarina design. Although still somewhat stodgy in appearance, it is a welcome alternative to the poorly-received Mondial coupé

With its substantial top folded, the Mondial Quattrovalvole Cabriolet is a satisfying open-air car. Rear seat room is minimal (as on the coupé) but headroom is no longer a problem! Rear vision is somewhat compromised by the high boot over the folded top

Several true spyder conversions of the 308GTS, with tiny fabric tops, have been built in Germany for Auto Becker

next gear with the fingertips but when you move it forcefully it goes in with absolute directness, telling you in a very mechanical way that, yes, by God, that's 3rd all right. Even if you don't use the gears religiously, the engine's flexibility lets you burble through traffic in a leisurely way.

'The steering has a direct, positive feel that some might find a little heavy. It's a bit slow for low-speed maneuvering, and the turning circle is rather large, but for fast road work it really does the job. There is a tendency toward understeer that increases as you go faster. This means you use a bit of muscle controlling the car but the big Michelin 240/55VR-390 tires have more grip than you're ever likely to use in normal spirited driving. There is oversteer at the very limit, as in our skidpad test (0.808g). Throwing the car from side to side in the slalom also makes the tail come out, and you have to keep the power on. The suspension is supple but noisy over sharp irregularities; you also get noticeable bump-steer from anything really protruding from the surface. The Cabriolet's structure is less rigid than the coupe's, transmitting some flexing and shaking.

'We now feel that Ferrari has a Mondial with real *raison de'être;*

faster, better looking, with wind-in-the-hair driving and all the attention from the sidelines you can handle. The Cabriolet was genuinely admired by most observers; drive it, and you will not be ignored. Forget the back seat, or put a Doberman in it as a guard dog. Two seats are enough, and the Ferrari has the performance to provide the most exhilarating open-air driving you could want.'

Again estimating the numbers of Mondial Cabriolets produced so far, we have a relatively small number of around 300 (still higher than any previous type of Ferrari soft-top) as of mid-1984. This brings the total of 246- and 308-based open cars into the approximate 7700 range, perhaps well over 8000 by the end of the year. From this we can see that the rarity factor of all the older Ferrari spyders and cabriolets will not be obtained when the current cars compete in future used-car markets. This is not to say that the GTS Targa style will not be more highly esteemed than the GTB—it almost certainly will be—but it cannot command the inflated prices of its predecessors. But this is good, because more Ferrari enthusiasts will have the opportunity of enjoying wind-in-the-hair motoring than ever before.

Dino and 308 spyders and cabriolets

Dino 246GTS	1180—beginning (Dino serial) 02132, ending 08518
308GT Rainbow	One—(Dino serial) 12788
308GTS	Approximately 1300—beginning 22619, ending 30687
308GTSi	Approximately 3300—beginning 31343, ending 41757
308GTSi Quattrovalvole	Approximately 1600 to date—beginning 41815, still in production
Mondial Quattrovalvole	Approximately 300 to date—beginning 47455, still in production

Approximately 7700 cars as of mid-1984

One-offs, rebodies and conversions

Having covered, more or less in chronological order, the Ferraris built originally as cabriolets and spyders, this book enters a vast grey area of modified cars. The modification of a Ferrari can be anything from a minor variation introduced at the time of body repair through completely new bodywork of different design. Between these two extremes fall the majority of the cars in this chapter, conversions of closed cars into cabriolets, spyders or Targas. In most cases the reason for a conversion was an almost totally destroyed original body, although in recent years it has become an accepted practice to cut off a perfectly good roof in order to have the more desirable open version.

In the mid-1960s Carrozzeria Fantuzzi built two new bodies over older chassis for NART. The first, on a 250GT 2+2 chassis, emulated the rear-engine 275P sports/racing car of 1964 in several of its details, including a low intake in the nose, headlights covered by contoured plastic fairings, a 'basket handle' type aerodynamic rollbar, and a recessed tail with a slight spoiler lip. Considering the relative bulk of the 2+2 chassis it was a reasonably successful exercise, though by no means handsome. A second Fantuzzi one-off was built with a 4-litre 330 engine; one of two cars reputed to have had the 1962 Le Mans-winning 330TRi chassis as its base, it certainly had an aggressive character, with a very long, low and penetrating nose, a low wraparound

plastic windscreen and a 'basket handle' airfoil, a bit too thin to be an effective rollbar. Painted gold, this Fantuzzi one-off was more likely built over a 330GT 2+2 chassis, as the production-type wheels and the left-hand (and fairly far forward) steering wheel position would seem to indicate. It did have such competition items as six carburettors, independent rear suspension and a five-speed gearbox, however.

Having formed his own business, Studio Tecnico Carrozzeria Giovanni Michelotti, in 1951, the former Vignale designer produced a number of prototypes for mass-produced cars but found time for several one-offs on Ferrari and other chassis. Among those were at least six spyders and cabriolets of original design, five of them for NART and one for Felber. The first, built in 1967 and on 330GT 2+2 chassis, was a rather ambitious yellow and black Targa that, aesthetically speaking, simply did not come off. Between 1974 and 1980 Michelotti built

Fantuzzi built this spyder on a 250GT 2+2 chassis for NART; its styling was inspired by the 275P prototypes of 1964

four spyders on 365GTB/4 Daytona chassis for NART. The first, shown at Turin in November 1974, was a reasonably well-chiselled variation on the Daytona form, except for heavy and unattractive black bumpers front and rear, and a leather-covered rollbar that resided under a full fabric top. At the Geneva Salon the following spring appeared a true Targa, a very Corvette-like white and red design that was intended for competition and actually entered for the Le Mans 24 hour race in June, but withdrawn.

The last two Michelotti spyders, in fact based on the last design begun by Giovanni Michelotti before his death, were the best of the lot. Of much cleaner conception than the previous two, the final design was completed by his son Eraldo in co-operation with Tateo Uchida, a member of the firm, and the first example was exhibited at the Turin Salon in the spring of 1980 before being shipped to Luigi Chinetti in the United States.

Above *Shown as the Felber Beach Car in 1976, this Michelotti one-off had no doors at all*

Top left *Another Fantuzzi conversion for NART was this spyder on a 4-litre chassis. It tried to emulate the 1962 Le Mans-winning 330TRi*

Bottom left *Michelotti built this strange Targa on a 330GT 2+2 chassis in 1967*

The last two 365GTB/4 NART spyders built by Michelotti in 1980 had this handsome wedge style

*Perhaps the most successful
rebody on a Ferrari chassis
was this extremely well
proportioned spyder by Neri
e Bonacini on a 250GT
chassis. It synthesized
250GTO and 275GTB/GTS
elements in a convincing
manner*

This car, and the second nearly identical example, were classic spyders with retracting fabric tops. Although certainly not better than the regular Pininfarina-designed, Scaglietti-built spyder, they had a slightly more modern, sharp-edged form with a prominent front airdam and wheel arches, the latter set off by the black-painted rocker panels. All in all, an attractive variation on the standard Daytona spyder.

An absolute one-off, to some extent a derivative of the 275GTB form but really an improvement on it, was the Neri e Bonacini spyder built on a 250GT chassis in 1966. With a very GTO-like nose and slimmer contours than those of the 275GTB, the design was one of the most impressive Ferraris ever, and certainly a refined expression of the mid-1960s idiom.

Having produced only six Ferrari bodies in the previous 24 years (a Panoramica-style berlinetta on 166MM chassis 0018 M in 1949 and five 250GT long-wheelbase berlinettas during 1956–1959), Carrozzeria Zagato SpA rebodied a 250GT as a spyder in 1971 and a 275GTS with a similar body in 1974. The 250-based car, called the 3Z (presumably for 3-litre Zagato) was yet another *pezzo unico* (one-off) for Luigi Chinetti, characterized by slotted headlight covers, disc wheels

The Zagato 3Z, built in 1971, was a rebody of a 250GT. The firm constructed this somewhat similar Targa in 1974, probably over a 330GTS chassis

and very large wheel arches. The 1974 example had similar contours but was a Targa with clear headlight covers and wire wheels. Zagato, like Touring, had its works in Milan to be near its main client, Alfa Romeo.

Built by Ferrari only as a coupé, the 365GTC/4 has recently become the subject of several cabriolet conversions, as well as at least one Targa. The first known cabriolet conversion was turned out by Luigi Chinetti Jr in 1981 and a second (for which the author

European Auto Restoration's handsome conversion of a 365GTC/4 into a cabriolet was completed in 1984

117

made the original sketches) was completed by European Auto Restoration at the beginning of 1984. The GTC/4 contours practically dictate where the new deck for the cabriolet must be, while the 365GTS/4 spyder provides a logical model for the top mechanism. The result is essentially what Pininfarina might have produced had Ferrari catalogued such a variation.

The making of a four-passenger Targa out of such a large car as the 365GT4 2+2 was a challenging project tackled by Fly Studio of Modena in 1976. Conceived by Ing. Giacomo Caliri, a former aerodynamicist at Ferrari,

Fly Studio in Modena built this interesting if not altogether successful Targa conversion of a 365GT4 2+2 in 1976

the project resulted in a T-bar roof, with removable panels on each side, and lengthened roof sails. The successors of the 365GT4 2+2, the 400A and 400i, have been the bases for several full cabriolet conversions; the best examples are probably those produced by R. Straman Company in California, but others have been completed by Coerper Auto Exclusiv of Düsseldorf and E G Autokraft (Restorations) Ltd in Ripley, Surrey. The 400 is a natural for cabriolet bodywork and again it is surprising that Pininfarina did not do a limited-production model.

On the other hand, the BB512 is a car for which a spyder conversion is not very logical. Soft-top BBs *have* been built, by Auto Becker and by Peter Lorenz in

As with the 308GTS in Chapter Five, a number of BB512 spyders were built for Auto Becker; this example was photographed at the Nürburgring in 1982

Overleaf Among the numerous open conversions by R. Straman are this BB512 Targa and 400i cabriolet, built in 1981

119

A BB512 conversion (compare page 119) was built by Lorenz in 1983. But note the longer engine cover

Germany and by Luigi Chinetti Jr in the United States; open-air Boxer motoring must be exhilarating in the extreme but the aesthetic solutions (especially with tops erected) are compromised by the short-hood, long-deck proportions. The same is true of several conversions of the 308GTS into soft-top spyders (again by Auto Becker), although the results are more successful with the close-coupled 308 chassis. And to come full circle, 308GTS-like Targa conversions have been made to BBs by several

122

Ferrari specialists. The styles, again almost completely dictated by the existing bodywork, have been predictable and for the most part handsome.

Two recent cabriolet conversions to large Ferrari 2+2 chassis were performed by Lazio Motor and Coach; on 330 and 365 chassis they are logical and successful transformations.

There is still one area of Ferrari open cars to be covered, that of projects designed by Ferrari but manufactured by other companies. The ASA 1000 was a small GT car that debuted in November 1961 with a 1032 cc four-cylinder engine designed at Maranello. The bodywork was a very neat berlinetta designed by Giorgio Giugiaro and built by Bertone. At least two cabriolets were built, the first exhibited at Geneva in 1963 with a fibreglass body. Unfortunately the company gave up the ghost in 1967.

Of longer duration, and more than serving its purpose in homologating a V6 engine that Ferrari wanted to run in Formula 2, was the Fiat Dino, produced in 2.0- and 2.4-

Two cabriolet conversions by Lazio include this 330GT 2+2 and 365GT 2+2, at least

Using a Ferrari-designed engine, the ASA 1000 was a Bertone design of which a cabriolet variation was shown in 1963

Powered by the Ferrari-built Dino V6 engine, the 1966 Fiat Dino spider had chunky Pininfarina bodywork

litre form between 1966 and 1973. A Pininfarina spider (Fiat's spelling) accounted for about one-fifth of the production run—1583 examples versus 6068 Bertone coupés. The spider's proportions were chunky at best, with high fenders and a very short hood, but it had an appeal all its own (stronger on the market than the handsome but sedate coupé) and remains an affordable alternative for the Ferrari enthusiast.

Specifications

166 Inter (1949–50)
Engine and transmission: Front-mounted, single-overhead camshaft, 60-degree V12; bore × stroke, 60 × 58.5 mm; displacement 1995 cc; compression ratio 7.5:1; one Weber 36 DCF carburettor; output 105 bhp at 6000 rpm; torque 12.8 kg/m at 5000 rpm; five-speed gearbox with synchros on 3rd, 4th and 5th; final drive ratio 4.66 or 5.00:1
Chassis and suspension: Tubular ladder frame; A-arms and transverse leaf spring front, live axle and semi-elliptic leaf springs rear; drum brakes; Borrani 15 in. disc or wire wheels; 5.90-15 tyres
Dimensions: Wheelbase 2500 mm; track 1270 mm front, 1250 mm rear; fuel capacity 90 litres; curb weight approximately 900 kg, according to bodywork
Cabriolet bodywork: Stabilimenti Farina (three); Vignale (one); Bertone (one)

212 Inter (1952–53)
As for 166 Inter, except:
Engine and transmission: Bore × stroke, 68 × 58.8 mm; displacement 2562 cc; compression ratio 7.5:1 (later 8.0); three Weber 36 DCF/3 carburettors; output 155 bhp (later 170) at 6500 rpm; torque 20.5 kg/m (later 21) at 5250 rpm
Chassis and suspension: Borrani 15 in. wire wheels; 6.40-15 tyres
Dimensions: Wheelbase 2500 or 2600 mm; track 1278 mm front; fuel capacity 105 litres; curb weight approximately 1000 kg, according to bodywork
Cabriolet bodywork: Vignale (six); Ghia (two); Pinin Farina (two); Touring (one); Abbott (one)

250 Europa (1954)
As for 212 Inter, except:
Engine and transmission: Bore × stroke, 68 × 68 mm; displacement 2963 cc; compression ratio 8.0:1; three Weber 40 DCF carburettors; output 200 bhp at 6000 rpm; torque 29 kg/m at 4500 rpm; four-speed all-synchro gearbox; final drive ratio 3.77, 4.25 or 4.75:1
Chassis and suspension: 7.10-15 tyres
Dimensions: Wheelbase 2600 or 2800 mm; track 1325 front, 1320 mm rear, fuel capacity 140 litres; curb weight approximately 1350 kg, according to bodywork
Cabriolet bodywork: Pinin Farina (one); Vignale (one, completed as 375 America, with 4522 cc, 300 bhp engine)

250GT (1955–56)

As for 250 Europa, except:

Engine and transmission: Bore × stroke, 73 × 58.8 mm, displacement 2953 cc; compression ratio 8.5:1; three Weber 36 DCZ/3 carburettors; output 220 bhp at 7000 rpm; torque 27 kg/m at 5000 rpm; final drive ratio 4.25, 4.57 or 4.86:1

Chassis and suspension: Coil springs front; Borrani 16 in. wire wheels, 6.00-16 tyres

Dimensions: Wheelbase 2600 mm; track 1354 mm front, 1349 mm rear; fuel capacity 95 litres; curb weight approximately 1050 kg, according to bodywork

Cabriolet bodywork: Boano (one)

342 America (1952–53)

Engine and transmission: Front-mounted, single-overhead camshaft, 60-degree V12; bore × stroke, 80 × 68 mm; displacement 4102 cc; compression ratio 7.5:1 (later 8.0); three Weber 40 DCF carburettors; output 200 bhp at 4800 rpm (later 5000); torque 37 kg/m at 3000 rpm; four-speed all synchro gearbox; final drive ratio 3.50, 3.62 or 4.00:1

Chassis and suspension: Tubular ladder frame; A-arms and transverse leaf spring front, live axle and semi-elliptic leaf springs rear; drum brakes; Borrani 15 in. wire wheels; 6.40-15 tyres

Dimensions: Wheelbase 2650 mm; track 1325 mm front, 1300 mm rear; fuel capacity 110 litres; curb weight approximately 1100 kg, according to bodywork

Cabriolet bodywork: Pinin Farina (two); Vignale (one)

410 Superamerica (1955–59)

As for 342 America, except:

Engine and transmission: Bore × stroke, 88 × 68 mm; displacement 4962 cc; compression ratio 8.5:1 (later 9.0:1); three Weber 40 DCF carburettors (later 42DCN and DCF); output 340 bhp at 6000 rpm (later 400 at 6500); torque 43 kg/m at 5000 rpm; final drive ratio 3.11, 3.22, 3.44 or 3.66:1 (later 3.34, 3.44, 3.56, 3.66, 3.76, 4.25, 4.57 or 4.86:1)

Chassis and suspension: A-arms and coil springs front; Borrani 16 in. wire wheels; 6.50-16 tyres

Dimensions: Wheelbase 2800 mm (later 2600); track 1455 mm front, 1450 mm rear; fuel capacity 100 litres; curb weight approximately 1200–1300 kg, according to bodywork

Cabriolet bodywork: Boano (one)

400 Superamerica (Series I, 1960–62)

As for 410 Superamerica, except:

Engine and transmission: Bore × stroke, 77 × 71 mm; displacement 3967 cc; compression ratio 9.8:1; three Weber 46 DCF3 carburettors; output 400 bhp at 6750 rpm; torque 42 kg/m at 4000 rpm; final drive ratio 3.77, 4.25 or 4.57:1

Chassis and suspension: Disc brakes, Borrani 15 in. wire wheels; 6.50-15 tyres

Dimensions: Wheelbase 2420 mm, track 1359 mm front, 1350 mm rear; fuel capacity 125 litres; curb weight approximately 1280 kg, according to bodywork

Cabriolet bodywork: Pininfarina (six); Scaglietti (two)

400 Superamerica (Series II, 1963–64)
As for 400 Superamerica Series I, except:
Engine and transmission: Compression ratio 8.8:1; three Weber 40 DCL/6 carburettors; output 340 bhp at 7000 rpm; torque 35 kg/m at 5000 rpm; final drive ratio 4.25:1
Chassis and suspension: Live axle with semi-elliptic and coil springs rear; 205-15 tyres
Dimensions: Wheelbase: 2600 mm; track 1395 mm front, 1390 mm rear; fuel capacity 90 litres; curb weight approximately 1450 kg, according to bodywork
Cabriolet bodywork: Pininfarina (four)

365 California (1967)
As for 400 Superamerica, Series II, except:
Engine and transmission: Bore × stroke, 81 × 71 mm; displacement 4390 cc; three Weber 40 DFI carburettors; output 320 bhp at 6600 rpm; torque 37 kg/m at 5000 rpm; five-speed all synchro gearbox
Dimensions: Wheelbase 2650 mm; track 1405 mm front, 1400 mm rear; curb weight approximately 1320 kg
Cabriolet bodywork: Pininfarina (14)

250GT Cabriolet (Series I, 1957–59)
Engine and transmission: Front-mounted, single-overhead camshaft, 60-degree V12; bore × stroke, 73 × 58.8 mm; displacement 2953 cc; compression ratio 8.5:1 (later 9.5); three Weber 36 DCZ3 carburettors; output 240 bhp at 7000 rpm; torque 27 kg/m at 5000 rpm; four-speed all-synchro gearbox; final drive ratio 3.66, 3.77, 4.00, 4.25 or 4.57.1
Chassis and suspension: Tubular ladder frame; A-arms and coil springs front, live axle and semi-elliptic leaf springs rear; drum brakes; Borrani 16 in. wire wheels; 6.00-16 tyres
Dimensions: Wheelbase 2600 mm; track 1354 mm front, 1349 mm rear; fuel capacity 95 litres (later 100); curb weight approximately 1150 kg
Cabriolet bodywork: Pinin Farina (four prototypes and 36 production cars)

250GT Cabriolet (Series II, 1959–62)
As for 250GT Cabriolet, Series I, except:
Engine and transmission: Compression ratio 8.8:1; torque 26.7 kg/m st 5000 rpm; final drive ratio 4.57:1
Chassis and suspension: Disc brakes; 175-400 tyres
Dimensions: Track 1350 mm rear; fuel capacity 90 litres; curb weight approximately 1200 kg
Cabriolet bodywork: Pininfarina (one prototype and 209 production cars)

275GTS (1964–66)
As for 250GT Cabriolet, Series II, except:
Engine and transmission: Bore × stroke, 77 × 58.8 mm; displacement 3286 cc; compression ratio 9.2:1; three Weber 40 DFI carburettors; output 260 bhp at 7000 rpm; torque 30 kg/m at 5000 rpm; five-speed all-synchro gearbox; final drive ratio 3.30 or 3.50:1.

Chassis and suspension: A-arms and coil springs rear; Borrani 14 in. wire wheels; 185-14 tyres
Dimensions: Wheelbase 2400 mm; track 1380 mm front, 1390 mm rear; fuel capacity 86 litres; curb weight approximately 1120 kg
Spyder bodywork: Pininfarina (203)

330GTS (1966–68)

As for 275GTS, except:
Engine and transmission: Bore × stroke, 77 × 71 mm; displacement 3977 cc; compression ratio 8.8:2; output 300 bhp at 7000 rpm; torque 33.2 kg/m at 5000 rpm: final drive ratio 3.44:1
Chassis and suspension: Campagnolo alloy disc wheels; 205-14 tyres
Dimensions: Fuel capacity 90 litres; curb weight approximately 1200 kg
Spyder bodywork: Pininfarina (100)

365GTS (1969–70)

As for 330GTS, except:
Engine and transmission: Bore × stroke, 81 × 71 mm; displacement 4390 cc; output 320 bhp at 6600 rpm; torque 37 kg/m at 5000 rpm
Dimensions: Curb weight approximately 1250 kg
Spyder bodywork: Pininfarina (20)

250GT Spyder California (long-wheelbase, 1958–60)

As for 250GT Cabriolet, Series I, except:
Engine and transmission: Output 260 bhp at 7000 rpm
Dimensions: Fuel capacity 140 litres; curb weight approximately 1100 kg (1000 kg with alloy body panels)
Spyder bodywork: Scaglietti (50)

250GT Spyder California (short-wheelbase, 1960–63)

As for 250GT Spyder California, long-wheelbase, except:
Engine and transmission: Compression ratio 9.2:1; output 280 bhp at 7000 rpm; torque 28 kg/m at 5500 rpm; final drive ratio 3.44, 3.55, 3.66, 3.77, 4.00, 4.25 or 4.57:1
Chassis and suspension: Disc brakes; 175-400 or 185-15 tyres
Dimensions: Wheelbase 2400 mm; fuel capacity 120 litres
Spyder bodywork: Scaglietti (75)

275GTB/4-S NART (1967–68)

As for 275GTS, except:
Engine and transmission: Twin-overhead camshaft, 60-degree V12; six Weber 40 DCN 9 carburettors; output 300 bhp at 8000 rpm; rear-mounted five-speed all-synchro gearbox in unit with differential; final drive ratio 3.55:1

Chassis and suspension: Campagnolo alloy disc wheels; 205-14 tyres
Dimensions: Track 1401 mm front, 1417 mm rear; fuel capacity 94 litres
Spyder bodywork: Scaglietti (ten)

365GTS/4 Daytona (1968–73)

Engine and transmission: Front-mounted, twin-overhead camshaft, 60-degree V12; bore × stroke, 81 × 71 mm; displacement 4390 cc; compression ratio 9.3:1; six Weber 40 DCN 20 carburettors; output 352 bhp at 7500 rpm; torque 44 kg/m at 5400 rpm; rear-mounted five-speed all-synchro gearbox in unit with differential; final drive ratio 3.30:1
Chassis and suspension: Tubular frame; A-arms and coil springs front and rear; disc brakes; Campagnolo 15 in. alloy disc wheels; 200/70VR-15 tyres
Dimensions: Wheelbase 2400 mm; track 1440 mm front, 1425 mm rear; fuel capacity 100 litres; curb weight approximately 1280 kg
Spyder bodywork: Scaglietti (136)

Dino 246GTS (1972–74)

Engine and transmission: Transverse rear-mounted, twin-overhead camshaft 65-degree V6; bore × stroke, 92.5 × 60 mm; displacement 2416 cc; compression ratio 9.0:1; three Weber 40 DCF 14 carburettors; output 195 bhp at 7600 rpm; torque 23 kg/m at 4800 rpm; five-speed all-synchro transverse gearbox in unit with differential; final drive ratio 3.82:1
Chassis and suspension: Tubular frame; A-arms and coil springs front and rear; disc brakes; Campagnolo 14 in. alloy disc wheels; 205/70VR-14 tyres
Dimensions: Wheelbase 2340 mm; track 1425 mm front, 1430 mm rear; fuel capacity 70 litres; curb weight approximately 1100 kg
Spyder bodywork: Scaglietti (1180)

308GTS (1977–80)

Engine and transmission: Transverse rear-mounted, twin-overhead camshaft 90-degree V8; bore × stroke, 81 × 71 mm; displacement 2927 cc; compression ratio 8.8:1 (USA 8.1:1); four Weber 40 DCNF carburettors; output 255 bhp at 7700 rpm (later 230 at 6600; USA 240 at 6600, later 208 at 6600); torque 30 kg/m at 5000 rpm (later 29 at 5000; USA 27 at 5000, later 25 at 5000); five-speed all-synchro transverse gearbox in unit with differential; final drive ratio 3.70:1
Chassis and suspension: Tubular frame; A-arms and coil springs front and rear; disc brakes; Campagnolo 5-spoke 14 in. alloy wheels; 205/70VR-14 tyres
Dimensions: Wheelbase 2340 mm; track 1460 mm front and rear; fuel capacity 80 or 74 litres; curb weight approximately 1340 kg (USA 1470)
Spyder bodywork: Scaglietti (approximately 1300)

308GTSi (1980–82)

As for 308GTS, except:
Engine and transmission: Bosch K-Jetronic fuel injection; output 214 bhp at 6600 rpm;

torque 24.8 kg/m at 4600 rpm; final drive ratio 3.70 or 4.06:1

Chassis and suspension: Optional 16 in. alloy wheels; 205/55VR-16 tyres front and 225/55VR-16 tyres rear

Dimensions: Fuel capacity 74 or 70 litres; curb weight approximately 1380 kg (USA 1525)

Spyder bodywork: Scaglietti (approximately 3300)

308GTSi Quattrovalvole (1982–84)

As for 308GTSi, except:

Engine and transmission: 4-valve cylinder heads; compression ratio 9.2:1; output 240 bhp at 7000 rpm (USA 230 at 6800); torque 26.5 kg/m at 5000 rpm (USA 26 at 5500); final drive ratio 3.82:1 (USA 4.06:1)

Dimensions: Curb weight approximately 1340 kg (USA 1435)

Spyder bodywork: Scaglietti (approximately 1600 to date)

Mondial Cabriolet Quattrovalvole (1984)

As for 308GTSi Quattrovalvole, except:

Engine and transmission: Final drive ratio 4.06:1

Chassis and suspension: 5-spoke 390-mm alloy wheels; 240/55VR-390 tyres

Dimensions: Wheelbase 2650 mm; track 1495 mm front and 1515 mm rear; fuel capacity 87 litres (USA 70); curb weight approximately 1500 kg (USA 1570)

Cabriolet bodywork: Scaglietti (approximately 300 to date)

Acknowledgements

A book of this type is mainly a compilation, and the author is indcbted to those who have helped assemble all the Ferrari material. Those who did the most are Gerald Roush of *Ferrari Market Letter*, Otis Meyer of the *Road & Track* library, Michael and Wilhelmina Sheehan of European Auto Restoration, Lee West of Newport Imports, Chuck Queener, Doug Nye, Jon Masterson and Luigi Chinetti.

The majority of the photographs are from Carrozzeria Pininfarina and the author; others were taken or supplied by (alphabetical order): Dean Batchelor, Studio Bertazzini, Carrozzeria Bertone, Peter Coltrin, Steve Dawson, Ferrari SpA SEFAC, Ferrari North America, Fiat Servizio Stampa, Ed Fisher, Geoffrey Goddard, Hiroshi Kitsune, Bernard Lemeunier, Scott Malcolm, Jon Masterson, Studio Moisio, Stanley Rosenthal, Joe Rusz, Alessandro Stefanini, R. Straman Co. and Kurt Wörner.

Index